SCOTT'S
GUIDE BOOK
TO THE SAMSUNG
GALAXY S20 SERIES

LEARN TO OPERATE YOUR SAMSUNG GALAXY S20, S20 PLUS AND S20 ULTRA WITH HIDDEN TIPS & TRICKS

SCOTT DOWNING

Goodwater Publishing
279 Stoney Lane
Dallas, TX 75212
Texas
USA

CONTENTS

CHAPTER 1
INTRODUCTION

Samsung in its annual *Unpacked* event on February 11, 2020 launched the Galaxy S20 series, consisting of the Galaxy S20, Galaxy S20+ and Galaxy S20 Ultra. The new Galaxy S20 series introduces a brand-new camera architecture that combines AI with Samsung's largest image sensor yet for stunning image quality. Along with the camera, the Galaxy S20 series makes the experience of everything we love to do with our phones, easier and better—enjoy personalized music for every moment of the day, watch videos the way they are meant to be seen and play console-style games on-the-go.

The Samsung Galaxy S20, Samsung Galaxy S20+, and Samsung Galaxy S20 Ultra are very similar. All the three phones have 120Hz displays, Qualcomm's Snapdragon 865 processor, expandable storage, water resistance, and wireless charging. This guide will assist you with all of the features and functionality of your new Galaxy S20 series. It also contains a lot of hidden tips and tricks to help you make the most out of your Galaxy S20 series.

GALAXY S20 SERIES FEATURES

Higher resolution camera sensors

The new Samsung Galaxy S20 series is designed with a brand-new camera architecture that combines AI with Samsung's largest image sensor yet for stunning image quality. The Galaxy S20 and S20+ have camera systems that consist of a 12-megapixel ultra-wide angle camera, a 12-megapixel wide-angle camera, and a 64-megapixel telephoto camera. The Galaxy S20+ model also has a fourth camera for depth-sensing. But it's the Ultra model that really stands out for its camera. The high-end model comes with a 108-megapixel wide angle camera, a 48-megapixel telephoto camera, a 12-megapixel ultra-wide-angle camera, and a depth-sensing camera. The 108 megapixels on the Ultra model are capable of grouping together to form a larger 12-megapixel sensor that can take in more light. The Samsung's

Galaxy S20 Ultra also has a higher resolution 40-megapixel selfie camera, while the other two models have a 10-megapixel front-facing camera.

Advanced zoom

In addition to having higher-resolution sensors, the Galaxy S20 series' camera can also zoom in further than other cameras. The Galaxy S20 and S20+ have an optical zoom of up to 3X and a digital zoom of up to 30X, while the Galaxy S20+ has an optical zoom of up to 10X and a digital zoom of up to 100X.

Single Take Mode

It's not just the camera hardware that Samsung changed with its Galaxy S20 series. The company also added a new feature called Single Take, which captures pictures in multiple formats with a single press of the shutter button. With Single Take, only tap the shutter and move around for at least 3 seconds and up to 10 seconds to capture the whole scene. Its revolutionary AI will give a variety of formats so that you can choose the best style for the moment without having to reshoot.

8K Video Snap

The new Samsung Galaxy S20 series are designed with a feature to capture still photography every time you hit record. It enables you to pull 33 MP pictures right from out of 8K high resolution video.

5G compatibility

The Samsung Galaxy S20 series is Samsung's first, full 5G flagship lineup. This means that all the Galaxy S20 models can connect to a 5G network, but only the S20+ and S20 Ultra can connect to the "fastest" (super-fast millimeter wave) 5G network.

All day battery

Samsung Galaxy S20 series are designed with powerful batteries that have a capacity range of 4000mAh to 5000mAh. Despite the high capacity rate, the Galaxy S20 series' batteries are also intelligent, adjusting to your mobile habits to save power and last way longer on a single charge.

Storage

Galaxy S20, S20+, and S20 Ultra are made for the powerful camera, with massive built-in storage to keep your high resolution videos and photos. You can then expand it with a microSD card for even more storage — up to 1.5TB total.

120Hz refresh rate

You can boost the Galaxy S20, S20+, and S20 Ultra's screen refresh rate up to 120Hz, which is higher than the average refresh rate of 60Hz on most smartphones. Boosting the refresh rate should make navigating the operating system and scrolling feel smoother and more natural.

Screen embedded fingerprint sensor

The new Samsung Galaxy S20 series have a fingerprint sensor embedded in the display, giving users a choice between unlocking their device through fingerprint or facial recognition.

Reverse wireless charging

Samsung Galaxy S20 series are designed with the Reverse wireless charging feature capable of wirelessly charging other devices by resting them on the phone's back.

GALAXY S20, GALAXY S20+ AND GALAXY S20 ULTRA COMPARISON

All three of the new Samsung Galaxy S20 series have a lot in common. They are quite similar in terms of design. From the front they look almost identical but dig deeper, there are some differences worth noting. The specs for the Samsung Galaxy S20 trio are compared side-by-side in the table below.

	Samsung Galaxy S20	Samsung Galaxy S20+	Samsung Galaxy S20 Ultra
Dimensions	151.7 x 69.1 x 7.9mm	161.9 x 73.7 x 7.8mm	166.9 x 76.0 x 8.8mm
Weight	163 grams	188 grams	222 grams
Colors	Cosmic Gray,	Cosmic Black,	Cosmic Black

	Cloud Blue and Cloud Pink	Cosmic Gray and Cloud Blue	and Cosmic Gray
Screen Display	6.2-inch WQHD+ Dynamic AMOLED display (120Hz)	6.7-inch WQHD+ Dynamic AMOLED display (120Hz)	6.9-inch WQHD+ Dynamic AMOLED display (120Hz)
Screen resolution	3200 x 1440 pixels	3200 x 1440 pixels	3200 x 1440 pixels
RAM	8GB / 12GB	8GB / 12GB	12GB/16GB
Storage	128GB; Expandable up to 1TB	128GB; Expandable up to 1TB	128GB/512GB; Expandable up to 1TB
Security	In-display fingerprint scanner (ultrasonic)	In-display fingerprint scanner (ultrasonic)	In-display fingerprint scanner (ultrasonic)
Operating System	Android 10	Android 10	Android 10
Processor	Qualcomm Snapdragon 865 / Samsung Exynos 990	Qualcomm Snapdragon 865 / Samsung Exynos 990	Qualcomm Snapdragon 865 / Samsung Exynos 990
Front Camera	10MP Selfie Camera	10MP Selfie Camera	40MP Selfie Camera
Rear Camera	Triple camera: 12MP Ultra Wide Camera, 12MP Wide-angle Camera and 64MP Telephoto	Quad camera: 12MP Ultra Wide Camera, 12MP Wide-angle Camera, 64MP	Quad camera: 12MP Ultra Wide Camera, 108MP Wide-angle Camera, 48MP

	Camera.	Telephoto Camera and Depth Vision Camera.	Telephoto Camera, and Depth Vision Camera.
Advanced Zoom	Hybrid Optic Zoom: 3x Super Resolution Zoom: up to 30x	Hybrid Optic Zoom: 3x Super Resolution Zoom: up to 30x	Hybrid Optic Zoom: 10x Super Resolution Zoom: up to 100x
Connectivity	LTE, 5G, NFC, Bluetooth 5.0, Wi-Fi, USB Type-C	LTE, 5G, NFC, Bluetooth 5.0, Wi-Fi, USB Type-C	LTE, 5G, NFC, Bluetooth 5.0, Wi-Fi, USB Type-C
Battery	4,000mAh, non-removable, 25W fast battery charging, fast wireless charging, reverse charging	4,500mAh, non-removable, 25W fast battery charging, fast wireless charging, reverse charging	5,000mAh, non-removable, 45W fast battery charging, fast wireless charging, reverse charging
Water Resistance	IP68	IP68	IP68

CHAPTER 2
GETTING STARTED

UNBOXING YOUR GALAXY S20 SERIES

What are the accessories that come with the Galaxy S20 Series? Make sure to look inside the box and take everything out. This is what is expected to come with your new Galaxy S20, Galaxy S20+ or Galaxy S20 Ultra:

1. **USB Cable**: Connect the USB-C to USB-C cable to the adapter to charge your phone.
2. **Travel Adapter**: A 25W charger adapter that you plug into an outlet.
3. **USB-C AKG headset**: A pair of headphones with a special USB-C port. All S20 models do not have a 3.5mm headset jack.

4. **Clear phone case**: A clear cover to help protect your phone from damage.

5. **Protective Film**: A clear screen protective film to help protect your screen from breakage.

6. **Extra earbuds**: The earbuds come in several different sizes. Swap them as needed so you can get the most comfortable fit.

7. **Ejector Tool**: Used for ejecting the SIM and microSD tray. All S20 models support a microSD card.

Please note that some of the listed components, including cover and protective film, may not be available depending on the model you purchase or the country or region you live in.

DEVICE LAYOUT

Galaxy S20 Layout

Front camera

Flash

Volume keys

Rear cameras

Side key

Fingerprint scanner

SAMSUNG

USB charger/Audio port

Galaxy S20+ Layout

Front camera

Flash

Volume keys

Rear cameras

Side key

Fingerprint scanner

USB charger/Audio port

Galaxy S20 Ultra Layout

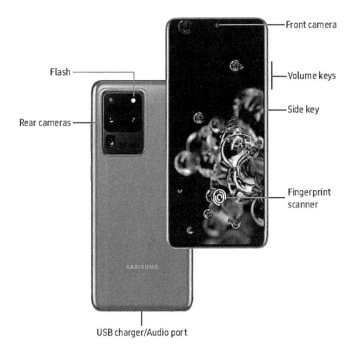

Flash

Rear cameras

Front camera

Volume keys

Side key

Fingerprint scanner

USB charger/Audio port

SET UP YOUR DEVICE

Your Galaxy S20/Galaxy S20+/Galaxy S20 Ultra device uses a nano-SIM card. A SIM card may be preinstalled, or you may be able to use your previous SIM card. Network indicators for 5G service are based on your carrier's specifications and network availability.

13

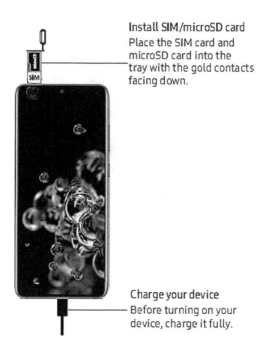

Install SIM/microSD card
Place the SIM card and microSD card into the tray with the gold contacts facing down.

Charge your device
Before turning on your device, charge it fully.

Charging the battery

It's very important that you charge the battery before using it for the first time or when it has been unused for extended periods. Always use only Samsung-approved battery, charger, and cable specifically designed for your device. This will help to maximize your battery life. Incompatible battery, charger, and cable can cause serious injuries or damage to your device. Use only USB Type-C cable supplied with the device. Follow the steps below to charge your Galaxy S20 series.

1. Connect the USB cable to the USB power adaptor.

2. Plug the USB cable into the device's multipurpose jack.

3. Plug the USB power adaptor into an electric socket.

4. After fully charging, disconnect the charger from the device. Then, unplug the charger from the electric socket.

Wireless PowerShare

You can wirelessly charge your compatible Samsung devices using your phone, but it's worthy to note that some features are not available while sharing power. Wireless PowerShare is a feature that turns the Galaxy S20 series device into a Qi wireless charger and charges other devices that support the standard, like the Galaxy Buds earbuds case, or even a smart Watch. It's best used in dire situations, as it's slow. To use the Wireless PowerShare feature, follow these steps to charge other compatible devices.

1. From Quick Settings, tap **Wireless PowerShare**.

2. With the phone face down, place the compatible device on the back of the phone to charge. A

notification sound or vibration occurs when charging begins.

For best results when using Wireless PowerShare, please note:

- Remove any accessories or covers before using the feature. Depending on the type of accessory or cover, Wireless PowerShare may not work properly.
- The location of the wireless charging coil may vary by device, so you may need to adjust the placement to make a connection. When charging starts, a notification or vibration will occur, so the notification will help you know you have made a connection.
- Call reception or data services may be affected, depending on your network environment.
- Charging speed or efficiency can vary depending on device condition or surrounding environment.

- Only devices that support the wireless charging feature can be charged using this feature. Some devices may not be charged.
- To charge properly, do not move or use either device while charging.
- If the remaining battery power drops below a certain level, power sharing will stop.
- Do not use headphones.

TURNING THE DEVICE ON AND OFF

Turning the device on

Press and hold the **Side** key for a few seconds to turn on the device.

When you turn on your device for the first time or after performing a data reset, follow the on-screen instructions to set up your device.

Turning the device off

1. To turn off the device, open the **Notification panel**, tap ⏻ **Power** and tap ⏻ **Power Off**. Confirm when prompted.

2. To restart the device, open the **Notification panel**, tap ⏻ **Power** and tap ⏻ **Restart**. Confirm when prompted.

You can also turn your device off by pressing the **Side** and **Volume down** keys at the same time.

INITIAL SETTING UP OF GALAXY S20 SERIES

When you turn on your device (whether Galaxy S20, Galaxy S20+ or Galaxy S20 Ultra) for the first time or after performing a data reset, the Setup Wizard guides you through the basics of setting up your device. Follow the prompts to choose a default language, connect to a Wi-Fi network, set up accounts, choose location services and more. After completing the setup, the Home screen will appear.

SET UP AND MANAGE YOUR ACCOUNTS

The accounts to be set up include Samsung account, Google account and Outlook account.

Add your Samsung Account

Your Samsung account is an integrated account service that allows you to use a variety of Samsung services provided by mobile devices, TVs, and the Samsung website. If you do not have a Samsung account, you should create one. You can create a Samsung account using your email address by following the steps below.

1. From **Settings**, tap 🔑 **Accounts and backup**
2. Select **Accounts**
3. Select ➕ **Add account** and tap 🔵 **Samsung account**.

Add your Google Account

Adding or setting up a Google account on your device will grant you access to your Google cloud storage, apps installed from your account and features like **Factory Reset Protection** (FRP). FRP prevents other people from using your device if it is reset to factory settings without your permission. For example, if your device is lost or stolen and a factory data reset is performed, only someone with your Google Account username and password can use the device. You can create a Google account by following the steps below.

1. From **Settings**, tap **Accounts and backup**.

2. Select **Accounts**.

3. Select ✛ **Add account** and tap on **Google**.

Add your Outlook Account

Signing in to your Outlook account will enable you view and manage your email messages. Follow the steps below to add your Outlook account.

1. From **Settings**, tap 🔑 **Accounts and backup**.

2. Select **Accounts**.

3. Select ✛ **Add account** and tap **Outlook**.

TRANSFER DATA FROM YOUR OLD DEVICE (SMART SWITCH)

Use Smart Switch to seamlessly transfer contacts, photos, music, videos, messages, notes, calendars, and more from your old device to your new Galaxy S20 series device. Smart Switch can transfer your data via USB cable, Wi-Fi, or computer.

Transferring data via USB cable

Follow these steps to transfer data from your old device using Smart Switch via USB cable

1. Connect the two phones as shown below using the old phone's USB cable. Make sure you've connected the USB-OTG adapter to the new Samsung Galaxy S20.

2. Launch **Smart Switch** on both devices by going to **Settings** and tap 🔑 **Accounts and backup**.

3. Tap **Send data** on the old device and tap **Cable**.

4. On your new Galaxy S20 Series, tap **Receive data**. Once it finishes scanning the old phone, select the data you want transferred, and then tap **Transfer**.

5. When the data transfer finishes, tap **Done** on your Galaxy S20 Series, and tap **Close** on the old device.

Transferring data wirelessly via Wi-Fi

Transfer data from your previous device to your device wirelessly via Wi-Fi Direct.

1. On the previous device, launch **Smart Switch**. If you do not have the app, download it from Galaxy Store.

2. On your device, go to **Settings** and tap 🔑 **Accounts and backup**, then select **Smart Switch**.

3. Place the devices near each other at about 4 inches apart.

4. On the previous device, tap **Send data** and select **Wireless**. The two devices will automatically connect.

5. On the previous device, select the item(s) you want to transfer and tap **Send**.

6. On your Galaxy S20 Series, tap **Receive**; the data transfer will begin.

7. When the transfer is complete, tap **Done** on your Galaxy S20 Series, and tap **Close** on your old device.

CHAPTER 3
USING YOUR DEVICE

NAVIGATING GALAXY S20 SERIES

The Galaxy S20/Galaxy S20+/Galaxy S20 Ultra comes with a touch screen that responds best to a light touch from your finger. Using excessive pressure or any sharp object on the touch screen may damage the touchscreen and void the warranty. When you turn on the screen, the navigation soft buttons will appear at the bottom of the screen. You may navigate your device by using either the navigation buttons or full screen gestures.

The navigation buttons are set to the **Recent apps** button, **Home** button, and **Back** button by default. The functions of the buttons can change according to the usage environment and may include:

- **Recent apps** button — Tap to open the list of recent apps.

- **Home** button — Tap to return to the Home screen.

- **Back** button — Tap to return to the previous screen.

Recent apps ——————— Back

Home

Setting Navigation bar options

Follow these steps to change how the navigation icons appear along the bottom of the screen.

- From **Settings**, tap ☀ **Display** and select **Navigation bar**. The following options are available:

  ○ **Navigation buttons**: Show the three navigation icons along the bottom of the screen.

    – **Button order**: Swap the order of the Back and Recent apps icons.

- ○ **Full screen gestures**: Hide the navigation icons for an unobstructed screen experience, and use screen gestures to navigate. The following options are available:

  – **More options**: Configure additional options for Full screen gestures.

  – **Gesture hints**: Display lines at the bottom of the screen where each screen gesture is located.

  – **Show button to hide keyboard**: Show an icon on the bottom right corner of the screen to hide the keyboard when the phone is in portrait mode.

Full screen gestures options

Follow these steps to customize your Full screen gestures even further by adjusting the sensitivity and enabling different types of gestures.

- From **Settings**, tap ☀ **Display** and select **Navigation bar**.
- Tap **Full screen gestures** and select **More options** for the following:
  - ○ **Swipe from bottom**: Swipe up from three different areas at the bottom of the screen to go

back, go to the Home screen, or view recent apps. You can also swipe up and hold the screen to use your device assistance app.

- o **Swipe from sides and bottom**: Swipe inward from either side of the screen to go back, swipe up from the bottom of the screen to go to the Home screen, and swipe up and hold the screen to view your recent apps.

  – **Back gesture sensitivity**: Drag the slider to adjust your device's sensitivity to detecting back gestures.

CUSTOMIZING GALAXY S20 SERIES HOME SCREEN

The Home screen is the starting point for accessing all of the device's features. It displays widgets, app icons, and more. You can set up additional Home screens, remove screens, change the order of screens, and choose a main Home screen.

App icons

You can launch an app from any Home screen by tapping on app icons. To add an app icon to the Home screen, follow the steps below.

1. From Apps screen, touch and hold the app icon you want to add to the Home screen and tap **Add to Home**.

To remove an icon from the Home screen:

2. Touch and hold an app icon on the Home screen, and tap **Remove from Home**.

Note that removing an icon from the Home screen does not delete the app; it only removes it from the Home screen.

Wallpapers

You can change the look of the Home and Lock screens by choosing a favorite picture, video or preloaded wallpaper.

1. From a Home screen, touch and hold the screen.
2. Tap **Wallpapers**.
3. Tap one of the following menus for available wallpapers:
    -   **My wallpapers**: Choose from featured and downloaded wallpapers.

- **Gallery**: Choose pictures and videos saved in the Gallery app.

- **Wallpaper services**: Enable additional features including guide page and Dynamic Lock screen.

- **Apply Dark mode to Wallpaper**: Enable to apply Dark mode to your wallpaper.

- **Explore more wallpapers**: Find and download more wallpapers from Galaxy Themes.

4. Tap a picture or video to choose it.

- If choosing a single picture, choose which screen or screens you want to apply the wallpaper to.

- Videos and multiple pictures can only be applied to the Lock screen.

5. Tap **Set on Home screen**, **Set on Lock screen**, or **Set on Home and Lock screens** (depending on which screens are applicable).

   • If applying a wallpaper to both the Home and Lock screens, enable **Sync my edits** if you want any edits made to that wallpaper to be applied to both screens.

Themes

Set a theme to be applied to your Home and Lock screens,

wallpapers, and app icons.

1. From a Home screen, touch and hold the screen.
2. Tap ⛳ **Themes** to customize.
3. Tap a theme to preview and download it to My themes.
4. Tap 👤 **My page** and select **Themes** to see downloaded themes.
5. Tap a theme, and then tap **Apply** to apply the selected theme.

Widgets

You can add widgets to your Home screen for quick access to information or apps.

1. From a Home screen, touch and hold the screen.
2. Tap ▦ **Widgets** and then touch and hold the widget that you want, drag it to the Home screen and release your hand.

Follow these steps to customize your added widget and how it will function.

- From a Home screen, touch and hold a widget, and tap an option:

o 🗑 **Remove from Home**: Delete a widget from your screen.

o ⚙ **Widget settings**: Customize the function or appearance of the widget.

o ⓘ **App info**: Review the widget usage, permissions, and more.

Home screen settings

The following settings and options will help you to customize your Home and Apps screens.

1. From a Home screen, touch and hold the screen.

2. Tap ⚙ **Home screen settings** to customize:

   • **Home screen layout**: Set your device to have separate Home and Apps screens, or only a Home screen where all apps are located.

   • **Home screen grid**: Choose a layout to determine how icons are arranged on the Home screen.

   • **Apps screen grid**: Choose a layout to determine how icons are arranged on the Apps screen.

   • **Apps button**: Add a button to the Home screen for easy access to the Apps screen.

- **App icon badges**: Enable to show badges on apps with active notifications. You can also choose the badge style.

- **Lock Home screen layout**: Prevent items on the Home screen from being removed or repositioned.

- **Add apps to Home screen**: Automatically add newly-downloaded apps to the Home screen.

- **Swipe down for notification panel**: Enable this feature to open the Notification panel by swiping down anywhere on the Home screen.

- **Rotate to landscape mode**: Rotate the Home screen automatically when your device's orientation is changed from portrait to landscape.

- **Hide apps**: Choose apps to hide from the Home and App screens. Return to this screen to restore hidden apps. Hidden apps are still installed and can appear as results in Finder searches.

- **About Home screen**: View version information.

Notification panel

For quick access to notifications, settings, and more, simply open the Notification panel.

Quick settings — Device settings

View all

Notification cards

View the Notification panel

You can access the Notification panel from any screen.

1. Drag the Status bar down to display the Notification panel.

2. Swipe down the list to see notification details.

    - To open an item, tap it.

    - To clear a single notification, drag the notification left or right.

    - To clear all notifications, tap **Clear**.

    - To customize notifications, tap **Notification settings**.

3. Drag upward from the bottom of the screen or tap ❬ **Back** to close the Notification panel.

LOCK OR UNLOCK YOUR DEVICE'S SCREEN

Pressing the **Side** key turns off the screen and locks it. Also, the screen turns off and automatically locks if the device is not used for a specified period. When the screen turns on, swipe in any direction to unlock the screen. If the screen is off, press the **Side** key to turn on the screen or alternatively, double-tap the screen.

Changing the screen lock method

You can choose from the following screen lock types that offer high, medium, or no security: Swipe, Pattern, PIN, Password, and None. It is recommended that you secure your device using a secure screen lock (Pattern, PIN, or Password). This is necessary to set up and enable biometric locks.

To change the screen lock method, follow these steps:

1. From **Settings**, tap 🔒 **Lock screen**.
2. Tap **Screen lock type** and select the desired method. The Screen lock types include the following:

- **Pattern**: Draw a pattern with four or more dots to unlock the screen.

- **PIN**: Enter a PIN with at least four numbers to unlock the screen.

- **Password**: Enter a password with at least four characters, numbers, or symbols to unlock the screen.

3. Toggle the **Notification** button **On** to enable showing notifications on the lock screen.

   The following options are available:

   - **View style**: Display notification details or hide them and show only an icon.

   - **Hide content**: Do not show notifications in the notification panel.

   - **Notifications to show**: Choose which notifications to show on the Lock screen.

   - **Show on Always On Display**: Display notifications on the Always on Display screen.

4. Tap **Done** when finished.

Using Face Recognition to unlock your screen

You can set the device to unlock the screen by recognizing your face. Before using the face recognition to unlock your device, you must bear in mind that face recognition is less secure than Pattern, PIN, or Password; and your device could be unlocked by someone or something that looks like your image. Secondly, some conditions may affect face recognition, including wearing glasses, hats, beards, or heavy make-up.

Follow the steps below to register your face:

1. Ensure that you are in a well-lit area and the camera lens is clean before starting the registration.
2. From **Settings**, tap **Biometrics and security**.
3. Select **Face Recognition** and follow the prompts to register your face.

Other options available to help you customize how face recognition works include.

- **Remove face data**: Delete existing faces.
- **Add alternative look**: Enhance face recognition by adding an alternative appearance.

- **Face unlock**: Enable or disable face recognition security.

- **Stay on Lock screen**: When you unlock your device with face recognition, stay on the Lock screen until you swipe the screen.

- **Faster recognition**: Turn on for faster face recognition. Turn off to increase security and make it harder to unlock using an image or video of your likeness.

- **Require open eyes**: Facial recognition will only recognize your face when your eyes are open.

- **Brighten screen**: Increase the screen brightness temporarily so that your face can be recognized in dark conditions.

- **Samsung Pass**: Access your online accounts using face recognition.

- **About unlocking with biometrics**: Learn additional information about securing your device with biometrics.

Using Fingerprint Recognition to unlock your screen

Use fingerprint recognition as an alternative to entering passwords in certain apps. You can also use your fingerprint to verify your identity when logging in to your Samsung account. To use your fingerprint to unlock your device, you must set a pattern, PIN, or password.

Follow the steps below to register your fingerprint:

1. From **Settings**, tap 🛡 **Biometrics and security**.

2. Select **Fingerprints** and follow the prompts to register your fingerprint.

Fingerprint management

This will enable you to add, delete, and rename fingerprints.

1. From **Settings**, tap 🛡 **Biometrics and security**.

2. Select **Fingerprints** for the following options:

   - The list of registered fingerprints is at the top of this list. You can tap a fingerprint to remove or rename it.

   - **Add fingerprint**: Simply follow the prompts to register another fingerprint.

   - **Check added fingerprints**: Scan your fingerprint to see if it has been registered.

Fingerprint verification settings

You can use fingerprint recognition to verify your identity in supported apps and actions.

1. From **Settings**, tap **Biometrics and security**.

2. Select **Fingerprints** for the following options:

    - **Fingerprint unlock**: Use your fingerprint for identification when unlocking your device.

    - **Show icon when screen is off**: Show the fingerprint icon when the screen is off.

    - **Samsung Pass**: Use your fingerprint for identification when using supported apps.

    - **Samsung Pay**: Use your fingerprints to make payments quickly and securely.

    - **About unlocking with biometrics**: Read details on the requirements each biometric security feature has for using your pattern, PIN, or password as a backup.

MOBILE CONTINUITY

Phone calls, messages, photo and video storage, and other functions of your device can be accessed and integrated across compatible mobile devices and computers using this feature. Mobile continuity feature can enable you to link your device to any Windows-based PC or by using Samsung DeX. You can also call and text on other devices using this feature.

Connecting your device to PC using Link to Windows

Linking your Galaxy S20 series phone and PC will enable you to easily sync pictures and much more directly to your computer. You can view your recent photos and send messages, or read texts on your phone and reply to them later on your computer. Additionally, you can manage notifications from apps and widgets without touching your phone.

To make linking your phone and PC as easy as possible, make sure you are signed into the same Microsoft account on your device as your PC. If you don't have a Microsoft account, make sure you create one.

Follow these steps to set up Link to Windows feature.

1. From **Settings**, tap **Advanced features** and select **Link to Windows**.

2. Toggle on **Link to Windows** to enable this feature.

3. Tap **Sign in with Microsoft**. Log into the same Microsoft account that's on your computer.

4. Tap **Continue** and allow the different permissions.

5. Follow the prompts to connect your device to your PC. Once you have successfully logged into your Microsoft Account on your Galaxy device, you will need to do the same on your PC.

6. Go to your **Windows Settings** and select **Account** on your PC (with Windows 10 or later).

7. Click **Sign in with a Microsoft account instead**.

8. Sign into the same Microsoft Account on your Galaxy S20 series device.

9. Once signed into your **Microsoft Account**, go to the **Microsoft Store**.

10. Search for your device (depending on the name you tagged your device) and click **Launch** to access your device.

11. Tap **Allow** on your Galaxy phone, so your device can connect to your PC.

Once they're linked, your phone and PC will share data with one another and you'll be able to easily access your texts, pictures, messages and notifications.

Connecting your device to PC using Samsung DeX

You can use Samsung DeX to connect your device to a PC for an enhanced, multitasking experience. This feature will help you achieve the following:

- Use your device and PC apps side-by-side.
- Share the keyboard, mouse, and screen between the two devices.
- Make phone calls or send texts while using DeX.

Follow these steps to Set up DeX on your PC:

1. Connect your mobile device to a PC with a standard USB-C cable.
2. Follow the instructions on your device for downloading and installing the DeX for PC software on your computer.

Call & text on other devices

This feature allows you to make and answer calls and text messages from your Galaxy S20 series devices that are signed in to your Samsung account.

1. From **Settings**, tap ☼ **Advanced features** and select **Call & text on other devices**.

2. Toggle on   **Call & text on other devices** to enable this feature. Connection occurs automatically.

3. Sign in to your Samsung account on your Galaxy S20 series devices. To access your contacts easily, move your contacts from your phone to your Samsung account.

MULTI WINDOW

Multi window feature on your Galaxy S20 series can multitask by using multiple apps at the same time. Apps that support Multi window can be displayed together on a split screen. You can switch between the apps and adjust the size of their windows.

Split screen control

Follow these steps to open an app in a multi window:

1. From any screen, tap ||| **Recent apps**.

2. Tap the app icon, and then tap **Open in split screen view**.

3. Tap an app in the other window to add it to the split screen view.

   - Drag the middle of the window border to adjust the window size.

EMERGENCY MODE

You can use Emergency mode to access helpful emergency

features and conserve your device's power during an emergency situation. To save battery power, Emergency mode:

- Restricts application usage to only essential applications and those you select.
- Turns off connectivity features and Mobile data when the screen is off.

Follow these steps to activate Emergency mode:

1. Open the **Notification panel**, and tap ⏻ **Power**.
2. Tap ⬛ **Emergency mode**.
   - When accessing for the first time, read and accept the terms and conditions.
3. Tap **Turn on**.

While in Emergency mode, only the following apps and features are available on the Home screen:

- **Flashlight**: Use the device's flash as a steady source of light.
- **Emergency alarm**: Sound an audible siren.
- **Share my location**: Send your location information to your emergency contacts.
- **Phone**: Launch the call screen.
- **Internet**: Launch the web browser.

- **Add**

  – Calculator: Launch the Calculator app.

  – Clock: Launch the Clock app.

  – Maps: Launch Google Maps.

  – Outlook: Launch the Outlook app.

  – Samsung Notes: Launch the Samsung Notes app.

- **Battery charge:** Displays estimated battery charge percentage.

- **Estimated battery life**: Displays estimated remaining battery charge time based on current battery charge and usage.

- **Emergency call**: Dial the emergency telephone number (for example, 911). This kind of call can be made even without activated service.

- **More options**:

  – **Turn off Emergency mode**: Disable Emergency mode and return to standard mode.

  – **Remove apps**: Choose apps to remove from the screen.

  – **Emergency contacts**: Manage your medical profile and ICE (In Case of Emergency) group contacts.

  – **Settings**: Configure the available settings. Only a

limited number of settings are enabled in Emergency mode.

Turn off Emergency mode

When emergency mode is turned off, the device returns to standard mode.

- Tap ⋮ **More options**, and tap **Turn off Emergency mode**.

CHAPTER 4
APPS

USING APPS

The Galaxy S20 series devices are preloaded with a number of Apps to enable you get the most out of your device. Apps can also be downloaded via the internet to your device during or after setup. Some of the Apps include but not limited to the following.

Phone	*Contacts*	*Messages*
Internet	*Camera*	*Gallery*
My Files	*Samsung Notes*	*Samsung Pay*

Installing apps

Apps may be purchased and downloaded from either Galaxy Store or Google Play Store. To install, launch the Galaxy Store or Google Play Store app. Browse apps by category or search for apps by keyword. Select an app to view information about it. To download free apps, tap **Install**. To purchase and download apps where charges apply, tap the price and follow the on-screen instructions.

Uninstalling or disabling apps

Installed apps can be removed from your device. Some apps that are preloaded (available on your device by default) can only be disabled. Disabled apps are turned off and hidden from the Apps list.

- From **Apps**, touch and hold an app, and tap **Uninstall/Disable**.

Enabling apps

1. Go to **Settings** and tap **Apps**.
2. Click on the **Down Arrow** and select **Disabled**.
3. Select an app and then tap **Enable**.

Sort apps

App shortcuts can be listed alphabetically or in your own custom order. Follow these steps to do that:

- From **Apps**, tap ⋮ **More options** and select **Sort** for the following sorting options:
  - **Custom order**: Arrange apps manually.
  - **Alphabetical order**: Sort apps alphabetically.

Create and use folders

You can make folders to organize App shortcuts on the Apps list.

1. From **Apps**, touch and hold an app shortcut, and then drag it on top of another app shortcut until it is highlighted.

2. Release the app shortcut to create the folder.
   - **Enter folder name**: Name the folder.
   - **Palette**: Change the folder color.
   - ┼ **Add apps**: Place more apps in the folder. Tap apps to select them, and then tap **Done**.

3. Tap ⟨ **Back** to close the folder.

Copy a folder to a Home screen

You can copy a folder to a Home screen.

- From **Apps**, touch and hold a folder, and tap ⬡ **Add to Home** icon.

Delete a folder

When you delete a folder, the app shortcuts return to the Apps list.

1. From **Apps**, touch and hold a folder to delete.

2. Tap 🗑 **Delete folder** icon, and confirm when prompted.

App settings

Manage your downloaded and preloaded apps. Options vary by app.

1. From **Settings**, tap ⚙ **Apps**.

2. Tap ⋮ **More options** for the following options:

   • **Sort by**: Sort the apps by size, name, last used, or last updated.

   • **Default apps**: Choose or change apps that are used by default for certain features, like email or browsing the Internet.

   • **Permission manager**: Control which apps have permissions to use certain features of your device.

   • **Show/Hide system apps**: Show or hide system (background) apps.

- **Special access**: Select which apps can have special access permissions to features on your device.

- **Reset app preferences**: Reset options that have been changed. Existing app data is not deleted.

3. Tap an app to view and update information about the app. The following options may be displayed:

Usage

- **Mobile data**: View mobile data usage.

- **Battery**: View battery usage since the last full charge.

- **Storage**: Manage the app's storage usage.

- **Memory**: View memory usage.

App settings

- **Notifications**: Configure notifications from the app.

- **Permissions**: View permissions granted to the app for access to your device's information.

- **Set as default**: Set the app as a default for a certain category of apps.

Advanced

- Options vary by app.

App info options

- **Open**: Launch the app. Not all apps have this option.

- **Uninstall/Disable**: Uninstall or disable the app. Some preloaded apps can only be disabled, not uninstalled.

- **Force stop**: Stop an app that is not working correctly.

PHONE

The Phone app is a very versatile tool in the device that can do more than just make telephone calls. This app can help you make calls, manage calls and explore nearby business and venues to get contact information and directions via Places.

CALLS

The Phone app allows you to make and answer calls from the **Home** screen, **Recents** tab, **Contacts** and more.

Access voicemail

Make a video call

Make a call

Make a call

Use your phone to make voice and video calls from a **Home** screen.

- From  **Phone**, enter a number on the keypad and tap **Call** to make a voice call or **Video call** to make a video call.

- Tap **Keypad** if the keypad is not displayed.

Enable swipe to call

You can enable swipe to make a call by swiping a contact or

number to the right.

To enable this feature, follow these steps:

- From **Settings**, tap ⚙ **Advanced features** and select **Motions and gestures**.

- Tap **Swipe to call or send messages**.

- Toggle on ⬤ to enable this feature.

Make a call from Recents

All incoming, outgoing, and missed calls are recorded in the Call log.

1. From ⓒ **Phone**, tap **Recents** to display a list of recent calls.

2. Tap a contact, and then tap ⬤ **Call**.

Make a call from Contacts

You can call a contact from the **Contacts** app.

- From ⬤ **Contacts**, swipe your finger across a contact to the right to call the contact.

Answer a call

When a call is received, the phone rings and the caller's phone number or name is displayed. If you are using an app, a pop-up screen is displayed for the incoming call.

- On the incoming call screen, drag 🔄 **Answer** to the right to answer the call.
- On the incoming call pop-up screen, tap 📞 **Answer** icon to answer the call.

Decline a call

You can choose to decline an incoming call. If you are using an app, a pop-up screen is displayed for the incoming call.

- On the incoming call screen, drag ⌢ **Decline** to the left to reject the call and send it to your voicemail.
- On the incoming pop-up screen, tap 📞 **Decline** to reject the call and send it to your voicemail.

Decline with a message

You can choose to decline an incoming call with a text message response.

- On the incoming call screen, drag **Send message** upward and select a message.

- On the incoming call pop-up screen, tap **Send message** and select a message.

End a call

- Tap ⌢ **End** when you are ready to end your call.

Actions while on a call

You can adjust call volume, switch to a headset or speaker, and even multitask while on a call.

Adjust call volume:

- Press the **Volume** keys to increase or decrease the volume.

Switch to headset or speaker:

Listen to the call using the speaker or through a Bluetooth headset (not included).

- Tap ◀)) **Speaker** to hear the caller using the speaker or tap ⅄ **Bluetooth** to hear the caller using a Bluetooth headset.

Multitask:

If you exit the call screen to use another app, your active call is indicated in the Status bar.

To return to the call screen

- Drag the Status bar down to display the Notification panel and tap the call.

To end a call while multitasking

- Drag the Status bar down to display the Notification panel, and then tap End call.

MANAGE CALLS

Your calls are recorded in a call log. You can set up speed dials, block numbers, and make a call with speed dial.

Call log

The numbers of the calls you have dialed, received, or missed are stored in the **Call log**.

- From 📞 **Phone**, tap **Recents**. A list of recent calls is displayed. If the caller is in your **Contacts** list, the caller's name is displayed.

Save a contact from a recent call

Use recent call information to create a contact or update your **Contacts** list.

1. From 📞 **Phone**, tap **Recents**.

2. Tap the call that contains the information that you want to save to your **Contacts** list, and tap ╋ **Add to contacts**.

3. Tap **Create new contact** or **Update existing contact**.

Delete call records

Follow these steps to delete **Call log** entries:

1. From 🅲 **Phone**, tap **Recents**.

2. Touch and hold the call you want to delete from the Call log.

3. Tap 🗑 **Delete**.

Block a number

By adding a caller to your **Block** list, future calls from this number are sent directly to your voicemail, and messages are not received.

1. From 🅲 **Phone**, tap **Recents**.

2. Tap the caller you want to add to the Block list.

3. Tap ⓘ **Details**, select ⃠ **Block**, and confirm when prompted.

Speed dial

You can assign a shortcut number to a contact for speed dialing their default number.

1. From 📞 **Phone** and tap **Keypad**.
2. Select ⋮ **More options** and tap **Speed dial numbers**. The Speed dial numbers screen displays the reserved speed dial numbers.
3. Tap an unassigned number.
   - Tap ▼ **Menu** to select a different Speed dial number than the next one in sequence.
   - Number 1 is reserved for Voicemail.
4. Type in a name or number, or tap 👤 **Add from Contacts** to assign a contact to the number.
   - The selected contact is displayed in the Speed dial number box.

Make a call with Speed dial

To make a call, tap and hold a speed dial number on the keypad from **Phone**. For speed dial numbers 10 and up, tap the first digit(s) of the number, and then tap and hold the last digit. For example, if you set the number 123 as a speed dial number, tap 1, tap 2, and then tap and hold 3.

Remove a Speed dial number

You can remove an assigned Speed dial number.

1. From **C** **Phone**, tap **⋮ More options** and select **Speed dial numbers**.

2. Tap **━ Remove** by the contact you want to remove from Speed dial.

PLACES

This feature helps you to discover the best restaurants and shops in your area. It allows you to find and contact nearby businesses from your Galaxy S20 series devices.

Follow these steps to use this feature.

1. From **C** **Phone**, tap **Places**.

2. Tap a category to search nearby.

3. Tap a location to view contact information and directions.

It's worthy to note that **Location services** must be enabled to use this feature.

OPTIONAL CALLING SERVICES

If available with your service plan, the following calling services are supported.

Place a multi-party call

If your service plan supports this feature, you can make another call while a call is in progress.

1. From the active call, tap ┼ **Add call** to dial the second call.

2. Dial the new number and tap 📞 **Call**. When the call is answered:

    *   Tap 🔲 **Swap** to switch between the two calls.
    *   Tap ⤳ **Merge** to hear both callers at once (multi-conferencing).

Real Time Text (RTT)

While on call with the other person, this feature enables you to type back and forth in real time. For this feature to work, the other person must have a phone that supports RTT or is connected to a teletypewriter (TTY) device. To differentiate this type of call from other calls, the RTT icon appears on all incoming RTT calls. Follow these steps to set up RTT call on your Galaxy S20 series devices.

1. From 📞 **Phone**, tap ⋮ **More options** and select **Settings**.

2. Tap **Real time text** for the following options:

- **Always visible**: Show the RTT call button on the keypad and during calls.

- **Use external TTY keyboard**: Hide the RTT keyboard when an external TTY keyboard is connected.

- **TTY mode**: Choose the preferred TTY mode for the keyboard in use.

CONTACTS

You can store and manage contacts on your device.

Create a contact

To create contacts on your device, follow these steps:

1. From Apps, select 👤 **Contacts** and tap ⊕ **Create contact**.

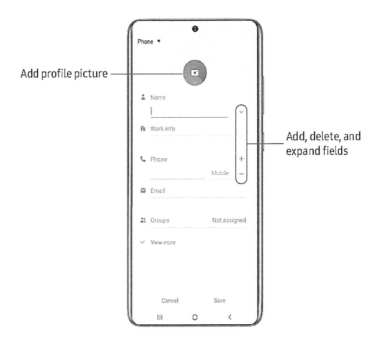

Add profile picture

Add, delete, and expand fields

2. Enter contact information and tap **Save**.

Edit a contact

When editing a contact, you can tap a field and change or delete information, or you can add more fields to the contact's list of information.

1. From **Contacts**, tap a contact.

2. Tap **Edit**.

3. Tap any of the fields to add, change, or delete information.

4. Tap **Save**.

Call or message a contact

You can quickly call or message a contact using their default phone number.

1. From **Contacts**, tap a contact.
2. Tap **Call** or **Message**.

Favorites

When you mark contacts as favorites, they are easily accessible from other apps.

1. From **Contacts**, tap a contact.
2. Tap **Add to Favorites** to mark the contact as a favorite.

To remove the contact from Favorites, tap **Favorite**.

Share a contact

You can share a contact on your Galaxy S20 series device with others by using various sharing methods and services.

1. From **Contacts**, tap a contact.
2. Tap **Share**.
3. Tap either **File** or **Text**.
4. Choose a sharing method and follow the prompts.

Create a group

You can use create your own contact groups in order to organize your contacts. Follow these steps to create your own group.

1. From 🔵 **Contacts**, tap ☰ **Open drawer** and select **Groups**.

2. Tap **Create group**, and then tap fields to enter information about the group:

   • **Group name**: Enter a name for the new group.

   • **Group ringtone**: Customize the sounds for the group.

   • **Add member**: Select contacts to add to the new group, and then tap **Done**.

3. Tap **Save**.

Add or remove group contacts

Follow these steps to add more contacts to a group, or remove contacts.

1. From 🔵 **Contacts**, tap ☰ **Open drawer** and select **Groups**.

2. Tap a group and do any of the following options.

- **To remove a contact**: Touch and hold a contact to select it, and then tap 🗑 **Remove**.

- **To add a contact**: Tap ✐ **Edit**, select **Add member**, and then tap the contacts you want to add. When finished, tap **Done** and select **Save**.

Delete a group

You can delete a group you have already created. To do so, follow these steps.

1. From 👤 **Contacts**, tap ☰ **Open drawer** and select **Groups**.

2. Tap a group and tap ⋮ **More options**.

3. Tap **Delete** and do any of the following options.

   - To only delete the group, tap **Group** only.

   - To delete the group and the contacts in the group, tap **Group and members**.

Import contacts

You can add contacts by importing them from other storages to your device as vCard files (VCF).

1. From 👤 **Contacts**, tap ☰ **Open drawer** and select **Manage contacts**.

2. Tap **Import or export contacts**.

3. Tap **Import** and select a storage location to import contacts from.

4. Tick contacts to import and tap **Done**.

Export contacts

You can manually back up your contacts to an installed memory card.

1. From ⊗ **Contacts**, tap ≡ **Open drawer** and select **Manage contacts**.

2. Tap **Import or export contacts**.

3. Tap **Export** and follow the prompts.

Delete contacts

You can delete a single contact or multiple contacts.

1. From ⊗ **Contacts**, touch and hold a contact to select it.

   - You can also tap multiple contacts to select them for deletion.

2. Tap 🗑 **Delete**, and confirm when prompted.

MESSAGES

Send a message

1. From **Apps**, tap 💬 **Messages** and select ⭕ **Compose new message**.

2. Add recipients and enter a message in the text input field.

3. Tap ◢ **Send** to send the message.

Send a message to a group

Send a text message to members of a group.

1. From 🧑 **Contacts**, tap ☰ **Open drawer** and select **Groups**. Then tap a group.

2. Tap ⋮ **More options** and select **Send message**.

Message search

To quickly locate a message, use the search feature.

1. From 💬 **Messages**, tap 🔍 **Search**.

2. Enter keywords in the **Search** field, and tap 🔍 **Search** on the keyboard.

Delete conversations

You can remove your conversion history by deleting conversations.

1. From 💬 **Messages**, tap ⋮ **More options** and select **Delete**.

2. Tap each conversation you want to delete.

3. Tap 🗑 **Delete**, and confirm when prompted.

Emergency alerts

This messaging feature enables you to be notified of imminent threats and other situations. There is no charge for receiving an 💬 ergency alert message.

1. From   **Messages**, tap   **More options** and select **Settings**.

2. Tap **Emergency alert settings** to customize notifications for emergency alerts.

Send SOS messages

You can send a message with your location to designated contacts when in an emergency situation.

1. Go to **Settings and** tap   **Advanced features**.

2. Select **Send SOS messages** and tap   to enable this feature.

3. Tap **Send messages to** and select **Add** to add recipients by creating new contacts or selecting from Contacts.

- To include a picture from your front and rear camera, tap **Attach pictures**.
- To include a five-second audio recording in your SOS message, tap **Attach audio recording**.

4. Press the **Side** key quickly three times to send an SOS message.

INTERNET

Browsing webpages

Samsung Internet is a simple, fast, and reliable web browser for your device. It enables you to securely browse the Web such browsing features as Secret Mode, Biometric Web Login, and Contents Blocker. Follow these steps to launch the browser.

1. From **Apps**, tap **Internet**.
2. Tap the address field.
3. Enter the web address or a keyword, and then tap **Go**.

Browser tabs

You can use tabs to view multiple web pages at the same time.

- From **Internet**, tap **Tabs** and select **New tab**.
  - To close a tab, tap **Tabs** and select ✕ **Close tab**.

Bookmarks

The Bookmarks page stores Bookmarks, Saved pages, and your browsing History.

Open a Bookmark

Follow these steps to quickly launch a web page from the Bookmarks page.

1. From **Internet**, tap ⭐ **Bookmarks**.
2. Tap a bookmark entry.

Save a web page

Saving a web page stores its content on your device so that you can access it offline.

1. Go to **Internet** and tap **Tools**.
2. Select **Add page to** and tap **Saved pages**.

- To view saved web pages, tap   **Tools** and select **Saved pages**.

View browsing history

Follow these steps to view a list of recently visited web pages: ◐   ≡

- Go to   **Internet**, tap   **Tools** and select **History**.
  - To clear your browsing history, tap ⋮ **More options** and select **Clear history**.

Secret mode

When in Secret mode, pages viewed are not listed in your browser history or search history, and as such there is no traces (such as cookies) on your device. Secret tabs are a darker shade than the normal tab windows.

1. From ◐ **Internet**, tap ⬒ **Tabs** and select **Turn on Secret mode**. Tap any of the following features for additional protection:
   - Smart anti-tracking
   - Ask sites not to track me
   - Lock Secret mode
2. Tap **Start** to begin browsing in Secret mode.

To turn off Secret mode:

- From ◯ **Internet**, tap 🔲 **Tabs** and select **Turn off Secret mode**.

CAMERA

You can capture high-quality pictures and videos using the **Camera** app. There are two ways to launch the Camera app: from Apps and from Quick launch (if enabled).

- From **Apps**, tap 🔲 **Camera**.
- If **Quick launch** is enabled, quickly press the **Side** key twice.

Take a picture

Follow these steps to take stunning pictures with your device's front and rear cameras.

1. From 🔘 **Camera**, set up your shot with the following features:

   - Tap the screen where you want the camera to focus.

     o When you tap the screen, a brightness scale appears. Drag the circle to adjust the brightness.

   - To quickly switch between the front and rear cameras, swipe the screen up or down.

   - To change to a different shooting mode, swipe the screen right or left.

   - To change camera settings, tap ⚙️ **Settings**.

2. Tap ◯ **Capture**.

Record videos

Follow these steps to record high-quality videos using your device.

1. From 🔘 **Camera**, swipe right or left to change the shooting mode to Video.

2. Tap   **Capture** to begin recording a video.

- To take a picture while recording, tap ⬚ **Capture**.

- To temporarily stop recording, tap ‖ **Pause**. To continue recording, tap • **Resume**.

3. Tap ▪ **Stop** when you are finished recording.

Configure shooting mode

Configuring shooting mode will allow the camera to determine the ideal mode for your pictures or choose from several shooting modes.

- From ⬚ **Camera**, swipe the screen right and left to change shooting modes.

  o **Photo**: Allow the camera to determine the ideal settings for pictures.

  o **Video**: Allow the camera to determine the ideal settings for videos.

  o **Single take**: Tap the shutter button to capture the scene in a series of pictures and short clips.

  o **More**: Choose other available shooting modes. Tap ✎ **Edit** to drag modes into or out of the Modes tray at the bottom of the Camera screen.

– **Pro**: Manually adjust the ISO sensitivity, exposure value, white balance, and color tone while taking pictures.

– **Panorama**: Create a linear image by taking pictures in either a horizontal or vertical direction.

– **Food**: Take pictures that emphasize the vivid colors of food.

– **Night**: Use this to take photos in low-light conditions, without using the flash.

– **Live focus**: Take artistic pictures by adjusting the depth of field.

– **Live focus video**: Record artistic videos with adjustable depths of focus.

– **Pro video**: Manually adjust the ISO sensitivity, exposure value, white balance, and color tone while recording videos.

– **Super slow-mo**: Record videos at an extremely high frame rate for viewing in high quality slow motion. You can play a specific section of each video in slow motion after recording it.

– **Slow motion**: Record videos at a high frame rate for viewing in slow motion.

– **Hyperlapse**: Create a time lapse video by recording at various frame rates. The frame rate is adjusted depending on the scene being recorded and the movement of the device.

Camera Features

Galaxy S20 series devices have several camera features that are designed to produce better and more professional pictures.

Super Slow-mo

This feature enables you record video at a high frame for viewing in high quality slow motion.

1. From **Camera**, swipe to **More** and then tap **Super slow-mo**.

2. Tap ● **Super Slow-mo** to record.

AR Zone

You can access all of your Augmented Reality (AR) features in one place.

- From **Camera**, swipe to **More**, and then tap **AR Zone**. The following features are available:
  - o **AR Emoji Camera**: Use the camera to create your My Emoji avatar.
  - o **AR Doodle**: Enhance videos by adding line drawings or handwriting to your environment. AR Doodle tracks faces and space so they move with you.
  - o **AR Emoji Studio**: Use AR tools to create and customize your My Emoji avatar.
  - o **AR Emoji Stickers**: Add AR stickers to your My Emoji avatar.
  - o **Deco Pic**: Decorate photos or videos in real time with the camera.
  - o **3D scanner**: Scan objects to create a 3D model. This is not available on the Galaxy S20 5G.
  - o **Quick measure**: Measure items in inches or centimeters using your camera. This is not available on the Galaxy S20 5G.
  - o **Home decor**: Virtually add appliances and furniture to a room to see how it will look in your space.

o **Makeup**: Preview makeup styles using the camera.

o **Styling**: Try on sunglasses using the camera.

Live focus

This camera feature helps you to add interactive focus effects to your pictures.

1. From ⬛ **Camera**, swipe to **More**, and then tap **Live focus**.

2. Tap ⬤ **Live focus effect**, choose an effect, and drag the slider to fine-tune the effect.

Live focus video

This feature enables you to create professional-looking films by applying background blurs and other special effects to your video. It cannot be used with zoom, Zoom-in mic, or Super steady.

1. From ⬛ **Camera**, swipe to **More**, then then tap **Live focus video**.

2. Tap ⬤ **Live focus effect**, choose an effect, and drag the slider to fine-tune the effect.

3. Tap ⬤ **Capture** to begin recording.

Zoom-in mic

This camera feature will help you to increase the volume of the sound being recorded and minimize background noise as you zoom in on an audio source. It cannot be used with Live focus video, Super steady, or with the front camera.

1. From **Camera**, tap **Settings** and select **Advanced recording options**.
2. Tap **Zoom-in mic**, and tap ⬤ to enable.
3. Tap ❮ **Back** to return to the main Camera screen.
4. Swipe to change the shooting mode to **Video**.
5. Tap • **Capture** to begin recording.
6. Bring your fingers together or apart on the screen to zoom in or out on the audio source. The microphone icon indicates the level of amplification being applied.

Scene optimizer

This camera feature automatically adjust exposure, contrast, white balance, and more based on what is detected in the camera frame to help you capture beautiful photos. The Scene optimizer is only available when using the rear camera. When activated, the Scene optimizer icon will change automatically based on what the camera detects, such as   when taking nature photos or   when taking photos in a dark setting. Follow the step below to activate this feature.

- From   **Camera**, swipe to **Photo**, and tap   **Scene optimizer**.

Super steady

Super steady applies advanced stabilization algorithms to your video for a smooth, professional appearance, even in heavy motion situations. This feature cannot be used with Zoom-in mic, Live focus video, Slow motion, or the front camera.

1. From 🔘 **Camera**, swipe to change the shooting mode to **Video**.
2. Tap ⊰🖐⊱ **Super steady**.
3. Tap • **Capture** to begin recording.

Camera settings

You can use the icons on the main camera screen and the settings menu to configure your camera's settings. This section will help you configure the camera's intelligent features, pictures, videos and other useful features.

- From **Camera**, tap **Settings** for the following options:

Intelligent features

- **Scene optimizer**: Automatically adjust the color settings of your pictures to match the subject matter.
- **Shot suggestions**: Get tips to help you choose the best shooting mode.
- **Smart selfie angle**: Automatically switch to a wide-angle selfie when there are more than two people in the frame.
- **Scan QR codes**: Automatically detect QR codes when using the camera.

Pictures

- **Swipe Shutter button to edge to**: Choose to either take a burst shot or create a GIF when you swipe the shutter to the nearest edge.
- **Save options**: Choose file formats and other saving options.
  - *HEIF pictures (Photo)*: Save pictures as high

efficiency images to save space. Some sharing sites may not support this format.

– *Save RAW copies*: Save JPEG and RAW copies of pictures taken in Pro mode.

– *Ultra wide shape correction*: Automatically correct distortion in pictures taken with the ultra wide lens.

Videos

- **Rear video size**: Select a resolution. Selecting a higher resolution for higher quality requires more memory.

- **Front video size**: Select a resolution. Selecting a higher resolution for higher quality requires more memory.

- **Advanced recording options**: Enhance your videos with advanced recording formats.

  – *High efficiency video*: Record videos in HEVC format to save space. Other devices or sharing sites may not support playback of this format.

  – *HDR10+ video*: Optimize videos by recording in HDR10+. Playback devices must support HDR10+ video.

– *Zoom-in mic*: Match the mic zoom to the camera zoom while recording videos.

- **Video stabilization**: Activate anti-shake to keep the focus steady when the camera is moving.

Useful features

- **Auto HDR**: Capture more detail in the bright and dark areas of your shots.

- **Selfie tone**: Add a warm or cool tint to your selfies.

- **Tracking auto-focus**: Keep a moving subject in focus.

- **Pictures as previewed**: Save selfies as they appear in the preview without flipping them.

- **Grid lines**: Display viewfinder grid lines to help compose a picture or video.

- **Location tags**: Attach a GPS location tag to the picture.

- **Shooting methods**:

– *Press Volume key to*: Use the Volume key to take pictures, record video, zoom, or control system volume.

– *Voice control*: Take pictures speaking key words.

– *Floating shutter button*: Add an extra shutter button that you can move anywhere on the screen.

– *Show palm*: Hold your hand out with your palm facing the camera to have your picture taken in a few seconds.

- **Storage location**: Select a memory location.

  – A memory card (not included) must be installed to view Storage location.

- **Shutter sound**: Play a tone when taking a picture.

- **Reset settings**: Reset the camera settings.

- **About Camera**: View app and software information.

GALLERY

Galaxy S20/Galaxy S20+/Galaxy S20 Ultra Gallery enables you to view, edit, and manage pictures and videos.

View pictures

You can view pictures stored on your device in the Gallery app. To view pictures, follow the steps below:

1. From **Apps,** tap ✳ **Gallery** and select **Pictures.**

2. Tap a picture to view it. Swipe left or right to view other pictures or videos.

   - To mark the picture as a favorite, tap ♡ **Favorite.**

   - Tap ◉ **Bixby Vision** to use Bixby Vision on the current picture.

   - To access the following features, tap ⋮ **More options**:

     – **Details**: View and edit information about the picture.

     – **Set as wallpaper**: Set the picture as wallpaper.

     – **Set as Always On Display image**: Set the picture as the background image for the Always On Display.

     – **Send as live message**: Use Live message to draw an animation on a picture and share it.

     – **Move to Secure Folder**: Move the picture to a Secure Folder.

     – **Print**: Send the picture to a connected printer.

Edit pictures

You can enhance your pictures using the Gallery's editing tools.

1. From ✹ **Gallery**, tap **Pictures**.
2. Tap a picture to view it, and then tap ✐ **Edit** for the following options:
   - ⬜ **Transform**: Rotate, flip, crop, or make other changes to the overall appearance of the picture.
   - ◎ **Filters**: Add color effects.
   - ☺ **Stickers**: Overlay illustrated or animated stickers.
   - T **Text**: Add text to the picture.
   - 🖌 **Draw**: Add handwritten text or hand drawn content.
   - ⬭ **Tone**: Adjust the brightness, exposure, contrast, and more.
3. Tap **Save** when finished.

Play video

You can view the videos stored on your device. You can also save videos as favorites, and view video details.

1. From ✹ **Gallery**, tap **Pictures**.

2. Tap a video to view it. Swipe left or right to view other pictures or videos.

- To mark the video as a favorite, tap ♡ **Favorite**. The video is added to Favorites under the Albums tab.

- To access the following features, tap ⋮ **More options**:

  - **Details**: View and edit information about the video.

  - **Set as wallpaper**: Set the video as wallpaper on the Lock screen.

  - **Move to Secure Folder**: Add this video to your Secure Folder.

3. Tap ▶ **Play video** to play the video.

Video enhancer

This feature enhances the image quality of your videos to enjoy brighter and more vivid colors.

1. From **Settings**, tap ✱ **Advanced features** and select Video enhancer.

2. Tap ◯ to enable this feature.

Edit video

This feature enables you to edit videos stored on your device.

1. From ✪ **Gallery**, tap **Pictures**.
2. Tap a video to view it.
3. Tap ✎ **Edit** to use the following tools:

   - ◯ **Rotate**: Rotate the video clockwise.
   - ✄ **Trim**: Cut segments of the video.
   - ◈ **Filters**: Add visual effects to the video.
   - ◙ **Portrait**: Enhance skin tones, eyes, and other facial features.
   - ☺ **Sticker**: Overlay illustrated or animated stickers.
   - ♪ **Audio**: Adjust the volume levels and add background music to the video.
   - ⊤ **Text**: Add text to your videos.
   - ✎ **Draw**: Draw on your video.
   - ◉ **Speed**: Adjust the play speed.

4. Tap **Save**, and confirm when prompted.

Delete pictures and videos

To delete pictures and videos stored on your device, follow these steps:

1. From ✳ **Gallery**, tap ⋮ **More options** and select **Edit**.

2. Tap pictures and videos to select them, or tap the **All** checkbox at the top of the screen to select all pictures and videos.

3. Tap 🗑 **Delete**, and confirm when prompted.

Share pictures and videos

You can share pictures and videos from the Gallery app. To do that, follow these steps.

1. From ✳ **Gallery**, tap **Pictures**.

2. Tap ⋮ **More options** and select **Share**. Then tap pictures and videos to select them.

3. Tap ⤳ **Share**, and choose an app or connection to use for sharing your selection. Follow the prompts.

Take a screenshot

This feature enables you to capture an image of your screen. Your device will automatically create a Screenshots album in the Gallery app. There are two ways you can take a screenshot of your screen and they are as follows.

- From any screen, press and release the **Side** and **Volume down** keys.

- **Palm swipe to capture a screenshot**: you can capture an image of your screen by swiping the edge of your hand across it, from side to side, keeping in contact with the screen. Follow these steps to enable this feature if it is not enabled.

    1. From **Settings**, tap **Advanced features** and select **Motions and gestures**.

    2. Tap **Palm swipe to capture** and tap ⟩ to enable this feature.

Screen recorder

This feature helps you to record activities on your device, write notes, and use the camera to record a video overlay of yourself to share with friends or family.

1. From **Quick Settings**, tap 🔴 **Screen recorder** to begin recording.

    - Tap ✏️ **Draw** to draw on the screen.

- Tap **Selfie video** to include a recording from your front camera.

2. Tap ⏹ **Stop** to finish recording. These are automatically saved to the Screen recording album in the Gallery.

MY FILES

You can view and manage files stored on your device, including images, videos, music, and sound clips. Follow this step to launch My Files.

- From **Apps**, tap **Samsung** folder and select ⬜ **My Files**.

Storage location ——

—— Search

File groups

Files stored in the device are organized into the following groups:

- **Recent files**: View recently accessed files.
- **Categories**: View your files based on the file type.
- **Storage**: View files saved on your device, optional SD card, and cloud accounts.

  – Cloud drives vary depending on the services you sign in to.

- **Analyze storage**: See what's taking up space in your storage.

My Files options

The options available on My Files can enable to search, edit, clear file history, and more.

- From **My Files**, the following options are available:

  - **Search**: Search for a file or folder.

  - **More options**:

    - **Clear recent files**: Remove the list of recently accessed files. This option is only available after a file has been opened through My Files.

    - **Analyze storage**: See what's taking up space in your storage.

    - **Trash**: Choose to restore or permanently remove files that you delete.

    - **Settings**: View settings for the app.

SAMSUNG NOTES

Samsung Notes are used to create notes containing text, images with footnotes, voice recordings, and music. Follow this step to create Samsung Notes.

- From **Apps**, tap **Samsung Notes** and select **Create**.

- When you finish adding texts, images, voice recordings and more; tap **Save**.

Access tools
Assign a category
Add an attachment
Set text options

Notes menu

You can view your notes by category.

- From  **Samsung Notes**, tap ≡ **Navigation drawer** for the following options:
    - o **All notes**: View all notes.
    - o **Frequently used**: Quick access to commonly used notes.
    - o **Shared notebooks**: View notebooks shared with your contacts through your Samsung account.
    - o **Trash**: View deleted notes for up to 15 days.
    - o **Categories**: View notes by category.

- ○ **Settings**: View settings for the Samsung Notes app.

- ○ **Manage categories**: Add, remove, and organize categories.

Notes options

You can edit, share, or manage notes.

1. From 🔲 **Samsung Notes**, tap ⋮ **More options** for the following options:

   - ○ **Edit**: Select notes to share, delete, or move.

   - ○ **Sort**: Change the way notes are organized.

   - ○ **View**: Switch between Grid, List, or Simple list.

Edit notes

Follow these steps to make edits to notes you already created. 🔲

1. From   **Samsung Notes**, tap a note to view it.
2. Tap ✏️ **Edit**, and make changes. When you are finished, tap **Save**.

SAMSUNG PAY

This app lets you make payments with your device. It is

accepted almost anywhere you can swipe or tap your credit card. A Samsung account is required. Follow these steps to launch Samsung Pay.

1. From **Apps**, tap **Samsung** folder and select **Samsung Pay**.

2. Tap **Get started** and follow the prompts.

Use Samsung Pay

Use Samsung Pay by opening the app and holding your device over the store's card reader.

1. From **Apps**, tap **Samsung** folder and select **Samsung Pay**.

2. Select a card to pay with and authorize payments by scanning your finger or by entering your Samsung Pay **PIN**.

3. Hold your phone over the store's card reader.

   • When your payment is complete, a receipt is sent to your registered email.

Simple Pay

You can use Simple Pay to access Samsung Pay from the Lock Screen, Home screen, or Always On Display. Follow these steps to activate Simple Pay.

1. From **Apps**, tap **Samsung** folder and select **Samsung Pay**.

2. Go to ☰ **Menu**, tap **Settings** and select **Use Favorite Cards**.

3. Tap ⬤ to enable Simple Pay on each screen.

To use Simple Pay:

1. From any screen, swipe up from the bottom of the screen.

   • Your payment card and Simple Pay are displayed.

2. Drag the card down to close Simple Pay.

CHAPTER 5
SETTINGS

There are two ways you can access your device settings and
they are as follows.

- Drag down the Status bar, and then tap ⚙ **Settings**.
- From Apps, tap ⊙ **Settings**.

CONNECTIONS

You can change settings for various connections, such as the
Wi-Fi feature and Bluetooth, between your device and a
variety of networks and other devices.

Wi-Fi

You can activate the Wi-Fi feature to connect to a Wi-Fi
network and access the Internet or other network devices
without using your mobile data.

To connect to a Wi-Fi network, follow the steps below.

1. From **Settings**, tap 📶 **Connections**, select **Wi-Fi** and tap ⬤ to activate it.

2. Scan for available networks and select a network from the Wi-Fi networks list. Networks that require a password appear with a lock icon. Enter the password and tap **Connect**.

3. Once the device connects to a Wi-Fi network, the device will reconnect to that network each time it is available without requiring a password. To prevent the device connecting to the network automatically, select it from the list of networks and tap **Forget**.

Manually connect to a Wi-Fi network

If the Wi-Fi network you want is not listed after a scan, you can still connect to it by entering the information manually.

1. From **Settings**, tap 📶 **Connections**, select **Wi-Fi** and tap ⬤ to activate it.

2. Tap ✛ **Add network** at the bottom of the list.

3. Enter information about the Wi-Fi network:

   - **Network name**: Type the exact name of the network.

- **Security**: Select a security option from the list, and enter the password if required.

- **MAC address type**: Choose which type of MAC address to use for this connection.

- **Auto reconnect**: Choose this option if you want to automatically reconnect to this network whenever you are in range.

- **Advanced**: Add any advanced options, such as IP and Proxy settings.

4. Tap **Save**.

Wi-Fi Direct

Wi-Fi Direct uses Wi-Fi network to share data between devices.

1. From **Settings**, tap 📶 **Connections**, select **Wi-Fi** and tap ◗ to activate it

2. Tap ⋮ **More options** and select **Wi-Fi Direct**. The detected devices are listed but if the device you want to connect to is not in the list, request that the device turns on its Wi-Fi Direct feature.

3. Select a device to connect to. The devices will be connected when the other device accepts the Wi-Fi Direct connection request.

Disconnect from Wi-Fi Direct connection

1. From **Settings**, tap 📶 **Connections** and select **Wi-Fi**.
2. Tap ⋮ **More options** and select **Wi-Fi Direct**. The device displays the connected devices in the list.
3. Tap the device name to disconnect the devices.

Bluetooth

You can use Bluetooth to exchange data or media files with other Bluetooth-enabled devices, like Bluetooth headphones or a Bluetooth-enabled vehicle infotainment system.

Pairing with other Bluetooth devices

Follow these steps to pair your device with other devices. Once a pairing is created, the devices remember each other and can exchange information without having to enter the passkey again.

1. From **Settings**, tap 📶 **Connections**, and tap 🅱 **Bluetooth**.

2. Tap ⬤ to turn on Bluetooth and the detected devices will be listed.

3. Select a device to pair with. If the device you want to pair with is not on the list, set the device to enter Bluetooth pairing mode.

4. Accept the Bluetooth connection request on your device to confirm. The devices will be connected when the other device accepts the Bluetooth connection request.

Rename a paired device

You can rename a paired device to make it easier to recognize.

1. From **Settings**, tap **Connections**, and tap **Bluetooth**.

2. Tap ⬤ to turn on Bluetooth.

3. Tap ⚙ **Settings** next to the device name, and then tap **Rename**.

4. Enter a new name, and tap **Rename**.

Unpair from a Bluetooth device

When you unpair from a Bluetooth device, the two devices

no longer recognize each other.

1. From **Settings**, tap 🛜 **Connections**, and tap ⓑ
   Bluetooth.

2. Tap ⬭ to turn on Bluetooth.

3. Tap ⚙ **Settings** next to the device, and then tap
   Unpair.

Dual audio

You can connect up to two Bluetooth audio devices to your
Galaxy S20 series devices.

1. Connect Bluetooth audio devices to your Galaxy S20
   series device.

2. From the Notification panel, tap ⏵ **Media**.

3. Under Audio output, tap ✅ next to each audio
   device to play audio to them (up to two devices).

Mobile networks

Mobile networks feature enables you to configure your
device's ability to connect to mobile networks and use
mobile data. To configure your device to use mobile data to
access internet, do the following:

- Go to **Settings**, tap   **Connections** and select **Mobile networks**.

Mobile hotspot

You can use mobile hotspot to share your device's mobile data connection with other devices through Wi-Fi network.

1. From **Settings**, tap 📶 **Connections**, select **Mobile Hotspot and Tethering**; and tap **Mobile Hotspot**.
2. Tap ▶ to turn on Mobile hotspot.
3. On the devices you want to connect, activate Wi-Fi and select your device's Mobile hotspot. Enter the Mobile hotspot password to connect.
   - To view a list of devices that are connected to your Mobile hotspot, tap **Connected devices**.

Change the Mobile hotspot password

You can customize your Mobile hotspot password to make it easier to remember.

1. From **Settings**, tap 📶 **Connections**, select **Mobile hotspot and tethering** and then tap **Mobile hotspot**.
2. Tap the password, enter a new password, and then tap **Save**.

Configure mobile hotspot settings

You can customize your mobile hotspot's security and connection settings.

1. From **Settings**, tap 🛜 **Connections**, select **Mobile hotspot and tethering** and then tap **Mobile hotspot**.

2. Tap ⋮ **More options** and select **Configure mobile hotspot** for the following settings:

   - **Network name**: View and change the name of your Mobile hotspot.

   - **Hide my device**: Prevent your Mobile hotspot from being discoverable by other devices.

   - **Security**: Choose the security level for your Mobile hotspot.

   - **Password**: If you choose a security level that uses a password, you can view or change it.

   - **Maximum connections**: Select how many devices can connect to your Mobile Hotspot at once.

   - **Power saving mode**: Reduce battery usage by analyzing hotspot traffic.

- **Protected management frames**: Enable this feature for additional privacy protections.

Tethering

You can use tethering to share your device's Internet connection with a computer.

1. From **Settings**, tap 🛜 **Connections** and select **Mobile hotspot and tethering**.
2. Tap an option:
   - Tap **Bluetooth tethering** to share your device's Internet connection using Bluetooth.
   - Connect the computer to the device using a USB cable, and then tap **USB tethering**.

Connect to a printer

You can connect your device to a printer via Wi-Fi network, and print images or documents. To use this feature, you have to add the printer plug-ins for printer(s) you want to connect the device to. Follow these steps to add printer plug-ins:

1. From **Settings**, tap 🛜 **Connections** and select **More connection settings**.

2. Tap **Printing** and select   **Download plugin** and follow the prompts to add a print service.

3. Tap the print service, and then tap ⁝ **More options**.

4. Select **Add printer**.

MirrorLink

If your car is compatible with MirrorLink, you can mirror your device's display on your car's entertainment and information screen using a USB connection.

1. Connect your device to your car's system using the USB cable.

2. From **Settings**, tap 📶 **Connections**, select **More connection settings** and then tap **MirrorLink**.

3. Tap **Connect to car via USB**, and follow the prompts.

DISPLAY

This feature enables you to configure the screen brightness, font size and other display settings.

Dark mode

Dark mode allows you to switch to a darker theme to keep your eyes more comfortable at night, darkening white or bright screens and notifications.

- From **Settings**, tap **Display**, and select one of the following options:

    o **Light**: Apply a light color theme to your device (Default).

    o **Dark**: Apply a dark color theme to your device.

    o **Dark mode settings**: Customize when and where Dark mode is applied.

    – **Turn on as scheduled**: Configure Dark mode for either **Sunset to sunrise** or **Custom schedule**.

    – **Apply to wallpaper**: Apply Dark mode settings to the wallpaper when it is active.

    – **Adaptive color filter**: Turn on Blue light filter automatically between sunset and sunrise to reduce eye strain.

Screen brightness

You can adjust the screen brightness according to lighting conditions or personal preference.

1. From **Settings**, tap **Display**.

2. Customize options under Brightness:

- Drag the **Brightness** slider to set a custom brightness level.

- Tap **Adaptive brightness** to automatically adjust the screen brightness based on the lighting conditions.

Motion smoothness

Get smoother scrolling and more realistic animations by increasing the screen's refresh rate.

1. From **Settings**, tap ☀ **Display** and select **Motion smoothness**.

2. Tap an option, and then tap **Apply**.

Blue light filter

The Blue light filter can help you sleep better if you use your device at night. You can set a schedule to automatically turn this feature on and off.

- From **Settings**, tap ☀ **Display**, select **Blue light filter**, and then choose one of the following options:

  o Drag the **Opacity** slider to set the opacity of the filter.

o Tap **Turn on now** to enable this feature.

o Tap **Turn on as scheduled** to set a schedule for
when Blue light filter should be enabled. You can
choose **Sunset to sunrise** or **Custom schedule**.

Screen mode

Your device has several screen mode options which adjust
the screen quality for different situations. You can select the
mode according to your preference.

1. From **Settings**, tap **Display** and select **Screen
mode**.

2. Tap an option to set a different screen mode.

Font size and style

You can change the font size and style to customize your
device.

- From **Settings**, tap **Display** and select **Font size
and style** for the following options:

o Drag the **Font size** slider to adjust the size of text.

o Tap **Font style** to choose a different font.

– Tap a font to select it, or tap **Download
fonts** to add fonts from Galaxy Store.

- Tap **Bold font** to make all fonts appear with bold weight.

Screen zoom

You can adjust the zoom level to increase or decrease the size of content on the screen.

1. From **Settings**, tap ☼ **Display** and select **Screen zoom**.

2. Drag the **Screen zoom** slider to adjust the zoom level.

Screen resolution

You can lower the screen resolution to save battery power, or increase it to sharpen the image quality. It's worthy to note that some apps may not support higher or lower screen resolution settings and may close when you change the resolution.

1. From **Settings**, tap ☼ **Display** and select **Screen resolution**.

2. Tap your preferred resolution, and then tap **Apply**.

Full screen apps

You can choose which apps you want to use in the full screen aspect ratio.

- From **Settings**, tap **Display** and select **Full screen apps** and tap apps to enable this feature.

Screen timeout

You can set the screen to turn off after a set amount of time.

- From **Settings**, tap **Display**, select **Screen timeout**, and tap a time limit to set it.

Accidental touch protection

Enabling this feature will prevent the screen from detecting touch input while the device is in a dark place, such as a pocket or a bag.

- From **Settings**, tap **Display** and select **Accidental touch protection** to enable or disable the feature.

Touch sensitivity

You can increase the touch sensitivity of the screen for use with screen protectors.

- From **Settings**, tap ☀ **Display** and select **Touch sensitivity** to enable.

Show charging information

The battery level and estimated time until the device is fully charged can be displayed when the screen is off.

- From **Settings**, tap ☀ **Display** and select **Show charging information** to enable.

Screensaver

You can set to display images as a screensaver when the screen turns off automatically or while the device is charging. ☀

1. From **Settings**, tap ☀ **Display** and select **Screen saver**.

2. Choose one of the following options:
   - **None**: Do not display a screen saver.
   - **Colors**: Tap the selector to display a changing screen of colors.
   - **Photo table**: Display pictures in a photo table.
   - **Photo frame**: Display pictures in a photo frame.

- **Photos**: Display pictures from your Google Photos account.

3. Tap **Preview** for a demonstration of the selected Screen saver.

Reduce animations

You can decrease certain motion effects, such as when opening apps.

- From **Settings**, tap ✦ **Advanced features** and select **Reduce animations** to enable the feature.

Lift to wake

You can turn on the screen by lifting the device.

1. From **Settings**, tap ✦ **Advanced features**, tap **Motions and gestures** and select **Lift to wake** to enable the feature.

Double tap to wake up

You can turn on the screen by double-tapping instead of using the Side key.

2. From **Settings**, tap ⚙ **Advanced features**, tap **Motions and gestures** and select **Double tap to wake** to enable the feature.

Smart stay

Smart stay feature uses the front camera to detect your face so that the screen stays on while you are looking at it.

- From **Settings**, tap ⚙ **Advanced features**, tap **Motions and gestures** and select **Smart stay**.
- Tap ⬤ to enable the feature.

One-handed mode

You can change the screen layout to accommodate operating your device with one hand.

1. From **Settings**, tap ⚙ **Advanced features** and select **One-handed mode**.
2. Tap **Use One-handed mode** to enable the feature and select one of the following options:
    - **Gesture**: Swipe down in the center of the bottom edge of the screen.
    - **Button**: Tap ⬜ **Home** two times in quick succession to reduce the display size.

NOTIFICATIONS

You can prioritize and streamline app alerts by changing which apps send notifications and how notifications alert you.

Manage notifications

You can configure notifications from apps and services.

- From **Settings**, tap **Notifications**.
  - **Suggest actions and replies**: Get applicable suggestions for actions to notifications and replies to messages.
  - **Show snooze option**: Get an option to snooze a notification for a later time.
  - **App icon badges**: Identify which apps have active notifications with badges that appear on their icons. Tap to choose whether or not badges indicate the number of unread notifications.

- ○ **Status bar**: Modify how many notifications appear on the Status bar.

- ○ **Do not disturb**: Block sounds and notifications while this mode is turned on. Specify exceptions for people, apps, and alarms.

- ○ To block notifications from an app, tap 🔘 next to the app. Tap **See all** to open the complete list of apps.

Customize app notifications

You can change notification settings for each app.

1. From **Settings**, tap 📷 **Notifications** and select **See all**.

2. Tap an app for the following options:

   - **Show notifications**: Receive notifications from this app.

   - **Categories**: Configure notification options that are specific to this app.

   - **App icon badges**: Show a badge on the icon when there are notifications.

Smart alert

You can set the device to notify you about missed calls and messages by vibrating when you pick it up.

1. From **Settings**, tap ✷ **Advanced features**, tap **Motions and gestures** and select **Smart alert**.

2. Tap ▶ to enable.

Smart pop-up view

You can receive notifications as icons that can be tapped and expanded in pop-up view.

- From **Settings**, tap ✷ **Advanced features**, and select **Smart pop-up view**.

- Tap ▶ to enable.

ACCESSIBILITY

Galaxy S20/Galaxy S20+/Galaxy S20 Ultra is designed to be used by everyone. If you have some kind of impairment, you can feel assured that this device has built-in Accessibility settings to make it easier to use. There are accessibility settings for people who need help seeing, hearing, or otherwise operating their device.

Screen Reader

Use special controls and settings that let you navigate without needing to see the screen.

1. From **Settings**, tap ⃛ **Accessibility** and select **Screen reader**.

2. Tap any of the options to activate the feature:

   - **Voice assistant**: Receive spoken feedback when using your device, such as what you touch, select, or activate.

   - **Tutorial**: Lean how to use Voice assistant.

   - **Settings**: Configure Voice assistant to better assist you.

Visibility enhancements

You can configure Accessibility features to assist with visual aspects of your device.

Colors and clarity

You can adjust the colors and contrast of text and other screen elements for easier viewing.

   - From **Settings**, tap ⃛ **Accessibility** and select **Visibility enhancements**. Tap any of the options:

     o **High contrast theme**: Adjust colors and screen fonts to increase the contrast for easier viewing.

o **High contrast fonts**: Adjust the color and outline of fonts to increase the contrast with the background.

o **High contrast keyboard**: Adjust the size of the Samsung keyboard and change its colors to increase the contrast between the keys and the background.

o **Show button shapes**: Show buttons with shaded backgrounds to make them stand out better against the wallpaper.

o **Colors inversion**: Reverse the display of colors from white text on a black background to black text on a white background.

o **Color adjustment**: Adjust the color of the screen if you find it difficult to see some colors.

o **Color lens**: Adjust the screen colors if you have difficulty reading the text.

o **Remove animations**: Remove certain screen effects if you are sensitive to motion.

Size and zoom

You can increase the size of supported screen elements and create shortcuts for accessibility features on your device.

- From **Settings**, tap 🧍 **Accessibility** and select **Visibility enhancements**. Tap any of the options:
  - ○ **Magnifier window**: Magnify content shown on the screen.
  - ○ **Magnification**: Use exaggerated gestures such as triple-tapping, double pinching, and dragging two fingers across the screen.
  - ○ **Large mouse/touchpad pointer**: Use a large pointer for a connected mouse or touchpad.
  - ○ **Font size and style**: Configure screen fonts.
  - ○ **Screen zoom**: Configure the screen zoom level.

Hearing Enhancements

You can configure Accessibility features to assist with audial aspects of the device.

Sounds

You can adjust audio quality when using hearing aids or earphones.

- From **Settings**, tap 🧍 **Accessibility** and select **Hearing enhancements**. Tap any of the options:

- o **Real time text**: Activate real-time text (RTT) calling.

- o **Hearing aid support**: Improve the sound quality to work better with hearing aids.

- o **Amplify ambient sound**: Enable this feature and connect headphones to your device to amplify the sounds of conversations.

- o **Adapt sound**: Customize the sound for each ear and enhance your listening experience.

- o **Mute all sounds**: Turn off all notifications and audio for privacy.

- o **Left/right sound balance**: Use the slider to adjust the left and right balance when listening to audio in stereo.

- o **Mono audio**: Switch audio from stereo to mono when using one earphone.

Text display

You can convert speech to text and watch closed captions when viewing multimedia.

- From **Settings**, tap 🧍 **Accessibility** and select **Hearing enhancements**. Tap any of the options:

- o **Live transcribe**: Use the microphone to record speech and convert it to text.

- o **Live caption**: Automatically caption speech in media played on your device.

- o **Subtitle settings**: Configure closed caption and subtitle services.

- o **Sound detectors**: Receive alerts when the device detects a baby crying or a doorbell.

Interaction and dexterity

Some people just function better when they use their hands. If you are one of those people, you can configure Accessibility features to assist with limited dexterity when interacting with your device.

Interactions

You can simplify the motions needed to answer phone calls or respond to notifications and alarms.

- • From **Settings**, tap ⛎ **Accessibility** and select **Interaction and dexterity**. Tap any of the options:

  - o **Answering and ending calls**:

    - – **Read caller names aloud**: Hear callers' names read aloud when using Bluetooth or headsets.

- **Press Volume up to answer**: Use the Volume keys to answer calls.
- **Answer automatically**: Answer calls after a set duration when using Bluetooth or headsets.
- **Press Side key to end**: End calls by pressing the **Power** key.

  o **Interaction control**: Customize areas of screen interactions, hardkeys, and the keyboard.

Touch settings

You can adjust your screen to be less sensitive to taps and touches.

- From **Settings**, tap Accessibility and select **Interaction and dexterity**. Tap any of the options:
  o **Touch and hold delay**: Select a time interval for this action.
  o **Tap duration**: Set how long an interaction must be held to be recognized as a tap.
  o **Ignore repeated touches**: Set a time duration in which to ignore repeated touches.

CHAPTER 6
GALAXY S20/S20+/S20 ULTRA TIPS AND TRICKS

The latest additions to Samsung's Galaxy S family, the Galaxy S20, S20+, and S20 Ultra, are packed with features and capabilities to help you do more, experience more, and pursue your passions. Here are some tips and tricks to enable you take advantage of it all.

How to change the Side key function

Unlike many other Android handsets, the Galaxy S20, S20+, and S20 Ultra all launch Samsung's Bixby virtual assistant by default when you press and hold the Side key. Thankfully, you can change the key's action so that it pulls up the power menu instead. Here's how.

1. From **Settings**, tap ⚙ **Advanced features** and select **Side key**.

2. Under the Press and hold heading, tap **Power off menu** option.

How to enable Always On Display (AOD) feature

Always On Display is a special feature available on Galaxy S20 series which helps you to view missed calls, messages alerts, check time and date without unlocking your device. To enable this feature, follow the steps below.

1. Go to **Settings**, and tap **Lock screen**.

2. Toggle the **Always On Display** option button to **On** to select any of the options.

   • **Display mode**: Customize when to show the AOD.

   • **Screen orientation**: Display the AOD in portrait or landscape mode.

   • **Show music information**: Show music details when the FaceWidgets music controller is in use.

   • **Auto brightness**: Automatically adjust the brightness of Always On Display.

- **About Always On Display**: View the current software version and license information.

3. Press the **back arrow** key to apply changes.

How to create movie from gallery

You can follow these steps to create a slideshow of your gallery content with video effects and music.

1. From ✳ **Gallery**, tap ▶️ **Create movie**.
2. Tap pictures and videos to add them to the movie.
3. Tap ▶️ **Create movie** and then choose either **Highlight reel** (automatic slideshow) or **Self-edited** (custom slideshow). The following options are available:

- ⏱ **Duration**: Adjust the run time of the entire movie (**Highlight reel** only).

- ⊟ **Transition effect**: Add visual interest to your movie by customizing the transitions between each clip (**Self-edited** only).

- ☰ **Title**: Add a title and a description to your movie.

- ♪ **Audio**: Adjust the volume of your movie, add sounds effects, or add music.

- ▷ **Clips**: View and edit each video or picture in your movie.
- ╀ **Add**: Incorporate additional clips from the gallery (**Self-edited** only).
- **Share**: Send your movie to friends and family.

4. Tap **Save**.

How to customize Galaxy S20 Series' Edge panels

You can customize the Edge panels.

1. From the Edge screen, tap ✿ **Settings**.
2. Tap ◗ to enable the feature. The following options are available:
   - ⦿ **Checkbox**: Enable or disable each panel.
   - **Edit** (if available): Configure individual panels.
   - ◌ **Search**: Find panels that are either installed or available to install.
   - ⋮ **More options**:

     – **Reorder**: Change the order of the panels by dragging them to the left or right.

     – **Uninstall**: Remove an Edge panel from your device.

     – **Handle settings**: Customize the position and

style of the Edge handle.

- **Galaxy Store**: Search for and download more Edge panels from Galaxy Store.

3. Tap ⟨ **Back** to save changes.

How to use the Quick Share feature

The Galaxy S20 series' Quick Share lets users share files with up to 5 friends at once with no device pairing required. Follow these steps to set it up.

1. Go to **Quick Setting** and long tap ⊙ **Quick share**.

2. Choose who may share files with you from the following options:

   - **Contacts only**: Only Samsung social users on your contacts can share things with you.

   - **Everyone**: Anyone nearby can share with you.

3. Set the device name by giving it an apt name so that it can be recognizable.

4. Make sure the Phone Visibility is enabled. If it is not, pull down the Quick Settings menu and tap on **Phone Visibility** to enable it or go to **Settings**, tap **Connections** and toggle on **Phone Visibility**.

To transfer files using Quick share:

1. The Quick Share option is on by default, but if not, activate it as above.

2. Choose the file(s) (video, pictures, documents) you would like to share and then tap **Share** icon.

3. At the top bar of the Quick share screen are listed the phones you can instantly share with, tap on the one(s) you want. You can share items with up to 5 friends simultaneously.

4. On the receiving device, ensure the screen is unlocked and you have **Accepted** the file transfer. The sharing will complete in seconds.

How to use the Music Share feature

Music Share is a particularly useful feature that lets your friends play music on your Bluetooth speakers. They don't have to set up their phones with Bluetooth speakers; instead, your Galaxy S20 series' device acts as the conduit for connecting your speakers with their phones. For example, you can play music stored on your friend's smartphone via your Bluetooth car stereo while keeping it and your Galaxy S20 series' device connected. Follow these steps to set it up.

1. From **Settings**, tap **Connections** and select **Bluetooth**.

2. Tap **Advanced** and toggle **Music Share** to **On**.

3. Tap **Music Share** to configure sharing options.

    - In the **Share devices with** setting, leave it to **Contacts only**. This way, only those in your contacts list will be able to use the feature.

    - You can set permissions from the **Ask for permission to connect** setting. Select from **Every time** or **Don't ask** based on your preferences.

    - **Disconnect when nothing is played for** ensures your Bluetooth devices aren't available all the time. You can choose between 5, 10, or 30 minutes, or you could just select **Don't disconnect** to have your devices always paired.

4. Once Music Share has been set up, all you need to do is connect to a Bluetooth speaker on your Galaxy S20 series. Then the device will show up on your contacts' Bluetooth speakers list, and they can just connect to it directly and start playing directly.

How to turn on Find My Mobile

Find My Mobile feature enables you to protect your device from loss or theft by allowing your device to be locked, tracked online, and for your data to be deleted remotely. A Samsung account is required, and Google location service must be turned on in order to use Find My Mobile. To turn it on and customize the options, follow these steps.

1. From **Settings**, tap 🛡 **Biometrics and security** and select **Find My Mobile**.

2. Tap ◗ to enable Find My Mobile and log in to your Samsung account. The following options are available:

    *   **Remote unlock**: Allow Samsung to store your PIN, pattern, or password, allowing you to unlock and control your device remotely.

    *   **Send last location**: Allow your device to send its last location to the Find My Mobile server when the remaining battery charge falls below a certain level.

How to change the device language

You can add languages to your list and organize them according to preference. If an app does not support your default language, then it will move to the next supported language in your list.

1. From **Settings**, tap ⬚ **General management**, tap **Language and input** and select **Language**.
2. Tap ✛ **Add language**, and select a language from the list.
3. Tap **Set as default** to change the device language.
   - To switch to another language on the list, tap the desired language, and then tap **Apply**.

How to use two separate accounts for the same app (Dual Messenger)

Dual Messenger capability lets you use two different accounts for the same app. That means you can keep your accounts for work and home separate, but on the same phone. Follow these steps to activate Dual Messenger on your device:

1. From **Settings**, tap ⚙ **Advanced features** and select **Dual messenger**.

2. Tap ⬤ next to supported apps to enable the feature for each app.

- To select which contacts have access to the secondary messenger app, tap **Use separate contacts list**.

How to reset Galaxy S20 series to factory settings

If you are having issues with your device, you may need to perform a Factory data reset. A Factory data reset will restore the device back to factory settings. This action permanently erases ALL data from the device, including Google or other account settings, system and application data and settings, downloaded applications, as well as your music, photos, videos, and other files. Any data stored on an external SD card is not affected. It is recommended that you save or backup important data before proceeding.

1. From **Settings**, tap ⚙ **General management** and select **Reset**.
2. Tap **Factory data reset**, tap **Reset** and follow the prompts to perform the reset.
3. When the device restarts, follow the prompts to set up your device.

How to know your device model, serial number and IMEI

You can view information about your device by following these steps:

1. From **Settings**, tap ⓘ **About phone** and then view your **phone number, model, serial number** and **IMEI** information.

2. Tap additional items to view more information about your device.

www.ingramcontent.com/pod-product-compliance
Lightning Source LLC
LaVergne TN
LVHW051245050326
832903LV00028B/2574